Explaining Baptism in The Holy Spirit

Dr. Mark W. G. Stibbe

Sovereign World

Bible quotations are taken from
the NIV The Holy Bible, New International Version.
© Copyright 1973, 1978, 1984 International Bible Society.
Published by Hodder & Stoughton.

ISBN: 1 85240 155 9

SOVEREIGN WORLD LIMITED
P.O. Box 777, Tonbridge, Kent TN11 9XT, England.

Typeset and printed in the UK by Sussex Litho Ltd, Chichester, West Sussex.

Contents

Christian life should begin with a conscious experience involving every level of the personality – not with a purely intellectual decision nor with a purely emotional event. The fundamental Christian experience, with its full content of conversion, regeneration, water baptism and reception of the Spirit... is worthy of being preached and practiced afresh in all its original power.

Siegfried Grossmann, 1977.

Preface

The doctrine of Spirit baptism has – in recent decades – spawned a good deal of discussion. Various phrases have been introduced in order to help us understand better the mystery of Spirit baptism – phrases like 'second blessing', 'release in the Spirit', 'completed initiation', and 'the actualisation of grace received in the sacrament of initiation'. As a result of these discussions, the whole subject of Spirit baptism has been advanced. This booklet attempts to further the discussion in a popular way, using many of the valuable insights from these recent studies.

Writing this book I have felt, at times, the weight of a great responsibility. I am now persuaded that the doctrine of Holy Spirit baptism could well turn out, in retrospect, to be the most important issue for the 20th century church. When the history books eventually get written, I suspect that this doctrine will be seen in terms comparable to the doctrine of justification by faith, which so transformed the church in the 16th and 17th centuries. To some, this may feel like an overstatement. To others, however, it will put the whole topic in its right perspective.

So it is with some due sense of trepidation that I offer this little book on the subject of Spirit baptism. I pray that the word 'Explaining' in the title will turn out to be justified. If it does, then it will in part be due to my students at the Department of Biblical Studies, Sheffield University. During my lecture course on 'The Holy Spirit in the New Testament' I have been greatly helped by their astute remarks. The months we spent together on the subject of baptism in the Spirit greatly helped to refine my own theology.

This book is therefore dedicated, with gratitude, to them.

1

Passages

There are few issues which divide Christians more quickly than 'baptism in the Holy Spirit'. Some ignore it, others adore it. Most are quietly confused about it. Whatever attitude we take, we must understand one thing: that Spirit baptism is a vital and consistent theme in the New Testament. John the Baptist talks about it. So does Jesus. So do Peter and Paul. If they say we need it, then we ought to desire it!

Let's look more closely at what John, Jesus, Peter and Paul actually said.

There are seven references to being 'baptised in the Holy Spirit' in the New Testament. Most of these contrast the ministry of John the Baptist with the ministry of Jesus. The difference between these two ministries of baptism centres upon the 'instrument' of baptism. The baptism of John is **in water**. The baptism of Jesus is **in the Holy Spirit and in fire**.

If we begin our study with what John the Baptist said, then our first port of call is Mark 1, verse 8. Here the language is (as always in Mark's gospel) brief and to the point. John says,

> *'I baptise you with water, but he* [i.e. Jesus] *will baptise you with the Holy Spirit'.*

In Matthew and Luke, the same saying is recorded in a more expanded form. Mark's tendency is to abbreviate sayings, so the longer version which we find in Matthew and Luke is almost certainly the full account of what the Baptist actually said:

> *'I baptise you with water for repentance. But after me will come one who is more powerful than I, whose sandals I am not fit to carry. He will baptise you with the Holy Spirit and with fire'.* (Matthew 3:11)

'I baptise you with water. But one more powerful than I will come, the thongs of whose sandals I am not worthy to untie. He will baptise you with the Holy Spirit and with fire'.

(Luke 3:16)

In these two texts, John makes it abundantly clear that Spirit baptism is to be a vital aspect of Jesus' ministry. John the Baptist warns his hearers of 'a More Powerful One' who is to come. Whereas he, John, baptises people in water for the cleansing of sin, Jesus will baptise people in the supernatural fire of God's Holy Spirit.

What of John's gospel? In John we find a slightly different emphasis. Here the interest of the author seems to be more in how the Baptist actually knew about Jesus' ministry of Spirit baptism – something which Matthew, Mark and Luke leave unsaid. In John 1:33, this gap is filled. Here the Baptist tells us that he received this knowledge in the form of a private revelation from 'the one who sent him' (i.e. God):

'I would not have known him [i.e. Jesus], *except that the one who sent me to baptise with water told me, "The man on whom you see the Spirit come down and remain is he who will baptise with the Holy Spirit".'*

Some time around 30AD, Jesus came to the river Jordan and was baptised by John in water. As he came up out of the water, Jesus was immersed in the power of God's Spirit. From that moment, the Holy Spirit 'remained' upon Jesus (John 1:33). As the charismatic Messiah of God, he was now given the power to baptise others in the Holy Spirit. So when did **that** happen? When did Jesus anoint his followers with the supernatural power of God?

The actual event happened about three years after the Baptist uttered his prophecy, on the great day of Pentecost. Shortly after his resurrection, and just before he was taken up into heaven, Jesus left his disciples with some final instructions:

'Do not leave Jerusalem, but wait for the gift my Father

promised, which you have heard me speak about. For John baptised with water, but in a few days, you will be baptised with the Holy Spirit'.   (Acts 1:4-5)

Not long after, the 120 disciples were all together in one place when the Holy Spirit came upon them with fire. They were all filled with the Spirit (Acts 2:4) and started to speak in tongues. As John foretold and as Jesus forewarned, they were truly 'baptised in the Holy Spirit and fire'.

The rest of Acts is a kind of a record of the 'Deeds of the Holy Spirit'. It is therefore not long before we find a sixth reference to Spirit baptism, at the point when the Gentiles are being converted and filled with the Holy Spirit (Acts 10). This is an unexpected turn of events because the first Christians were all Jews. Some explanation is therefore required. So in Acts 11 Peter goes to the church leaders in Jerusalem and describes how the Holy Spirit fell on the Gentiles as he was preaching. This is what Peter declares:

'As I began to speak, the Holy Spirit came on them as he had come on us at the beginning. Then I remembered what the Lord had said: "John baptised with water, but you will be baptised with the Holy Spirit". So if God gave them the same gift as he gave us, who believed in the Lord Jesus Christ, who was I to think that I could oppose God?'

(Acts 11:15-17)

The important thing here is Peter's acknowledgement that the Gentiles had experienced the same Spirit baptism which he and the 119 had experienced on the Day of Pentecost. Peter now realises that both Jews and Gentiles can repent of sin, come to faith in Christ, and receive the gift of the Spirit. Anyone can be baptised in the Holy Spirit. Young and old, men and women, Jews and Gentiles, all can be filled with the Spirit:

'In the last days, God says, I will pour out my Spirit on all people. Your sons and daughters will prophesy, your young men will see visions, your old men will dream dreams. Even on my servants, both men and women, I will pour out my

Spirit in those days, and they will prophesy.' (Acts 2:17-18)

The days after Pentecost therefore constitute a new age of the Spirit. The last days have dawned, and a new democracy of the Spirit has arrived – a democracy in which all can be baptised in the Holy Spirit of God.

This thought is given an extra emphasis in the seventh and final reference to Spirit baptism in the New Testament. This is not in the Gospels and Acts but in Paul's first letter to the Corinthians. In chapter 12 verse 13, Paul reminds the church members in Corinth that there is no room for elitism in the church. Why? Because they all came into the church the same way. They were all baptised in the same Spirit:

> *'For we were all baptised in one Spirit into one body – whether Jews or Greeks, slave or free – and we were all given the one Spirit to drink'.*

In these words Paul makes explicit reference to baptism in the Holy Spirit. Indeed, he uses the same construction which we find in the other six references: 'baptised in or by the Spirit' (*en eni pneumati... ebaptisthemen*). The only difference is that Paul talks about being baptised in 'one Spirit' whilst the other six references talk about being baptised in 'Holy Spirit' (*baptisei... en pneumati hagio*).

So looking at the New Testament as a whole, a picture emerges of the historical development of the concept of baptism in the Holy Spirit. From our seven passages we can conclude the following:

Stage 1. In about 30AD, John the Baptist hears a word of revelation from God: *'The man on whom you see the Spirit come down and remain is he who will baptise with the Holy Spirit.'* (John 1:33)

Stage 2: John the Baptist, from the basis of this revelation, starts to preach in these words: *'I baptise you with water for repentance. But after me will come one who is more powerful* *than I, whose sandals I am not fit to carry. He will baptise you with the Holy Spirit and with fire.'* (Matthew 3:11/Luke 3:16)

Stage 3: Not long after, Jesus comes to the River Jordan to be baptised by John. As Jesus comes up from the water, the Holy Spirit comes down from heaven. Jesus is baptised in the Holy Spirit before John's very eyes. The prophetic word which John had been given in stage 1 is now beginning to be fulfilled.

Stage 4: Three years later (circa 33AD), just before he is taken up into heaven, Jesus reminds his followers of John the Baptist's prophecy and tells them to wait for the Spirit baptism which he himself will administer to them (Acts 1:4-5).

Stage 5: Again, as in stage 3, Jesus goes up and the Spirit comes down! This time Jesus ascends to heaven and from there sends the Holy Spirit down upon the disciples. On the Day of Pentecost, the 120 disciples are baptised in the Holy Spirit. It is truly a watershed experience!

Stage 6: After the 120 disciples are baptised in the Holy Spirit on the Day of Pentecost, the apostles find that others, even Gentiles, are filled with the Holy Spirit. This experience is duly interpreted in the light of John the Baptist's prophecy and is regarded as 'baptism in the Holy Spirit' (Acts 11:15-17).

Stage 7: By the 50s AD (when 1 Corinthians was written), Paul can refer to the experience of becoming a member of Christ's body, the church as being 'baptised in one Spirit into one body'.

Summing up: there are seven references to being 'baptised in (the) Holy Spirit' in the New Testament. Six of these references contrast the ministry of John the Baptist (water baptism) with the ministry of Jesus (Spirit baptism). These are:

> Mark 1:8
> Matthew 3:11
> Luke 3:16

John 1:33
Acts 1:4-5
Acts 11:15-17

The seventh reference is in 1 Corinthians 12:13, where Paul talks about Spirit baptism as the means by which all believers become members of the Body of Christ.

2

Profile

So what is this 'baptism in the Holy Spirit'? What kind of experiences were John the Baptist, Jesus, Peter and Paul referring to when they used this phrase?

To define this concept accurately, we need to begin with a careful examination of the word 'baptise'. As the reader will probably be aware, the New Testament was not originally written in English but in a kind of popular Greek. So it is to the original Greek words that we must turn for a full understanding of our subject.

In all seven passages referred to above, the word translated 'baptised' comes from the Greek verb *baptizo* ('I baptise'). *Baptizo* is a longer form of the verb *bapto* meaning 'I dip'. *Bapto* was used particularly frequently in the context of dyeing clothes. Whenever someone wove a garment out of different materials of roughly the same colour, the natural colours of those materials created a patchwork of diverse hues. In other words, the colour of the whole garment was not uniform. The garment had to be dipped in a colour dye if it was to have a uniform density of shade. When that happened, the verb used was *bapto*, 'I dip'.

Baptizo is an intensive form of the verb *bapto*. That is to say, it is a word which was developed in order to emphasise the note of total immersion. It was sometimes used for the dyeing process (dipping clothes in a total sense). A garment that was dyed in every aspect was therefore said to be 'baptised'. At other times it was used of a drowning man. Someone who lost his life by drowning was also said to have been 'baptised', totally immersed in water. On still other occasions it was used of a ship which sunk at sea. Such a vessel, once it was completely submerged and saturated, would be described as 'baptised'.

There are three main reasons why the New Testament uses this verb *baptizein* to describe the believer's reception of the gift of the Holy Spirit.

First, one important thing about being baptised is this: it is not something which I can do to myself. It is something which someone must do to me. This is obviously true for water baptism, where I require an authorised minister of the Church to immerse me in the baptismal waters. In the case of Spirit baptism, this is even more true. To be baptised in the Holy Spirit, I need the help of the Lord Jesus. Jesus is the subject, we – his disciples – are the object, and the Holy Spirit is the instrument. It is therefore an event in which we are the recipients not the initiators. We receive baptism in the Holy Spirit from the risen, Ascended Lord Jesus. It is Jesus, ascended and glorified in heaven, who baptises us in Holy Spirit (see Ephesians 3:7-8). Consequently, we are like the garment mentioned above. We do not immerse ourselves. The Lord Jesus immerses us!

Secondly, Spirit baptism is not just an anointing on part of our lives. It is a matter of total saturation. Like the garment made up of many materials, we are completely immersed in one overwhelming reality. From that moment on, every part of our lives is uniformly energised by the Spirit of the Living God. The reason why the New Testament teachers use the word 'baptise' is because they are talking about an overwhelming and all-embracing experience. Spirit baptism is not a dipping of part of our lives in the Spirit. It is a total experience!

Thirdly, the use of the verb 'baptise' emphasises that the event is to do with initiation – with our Christian birth, as it were. There is a rather obvious point which is never really made here, and this is as follows: no one doubts that the word 'baptism', when used in connection with water, refers to our initiation as Christian disciples. Water baptism is the outward sign that we have died to sin and risen to life in Christ. It is a sacrament which, amongst other things, marks the fact that we have started on the Way. This connotation of 'initiation' applies also to baptism in the Holy Spirit. By choosing to use the verb *baptizein* of our reception of the gift of the Spirit, the New Testament is implying that this too has something to do with initiation into Christ. To be sure, other phrases are used in Acts to describe the believer's experience of the presence and the power of the Spirit:

14

a) Sometimes the Holy Spirit is said to *'come upon'* people (Acts 1:8; 19:6);
b) Sometimes people are said to *'be filled by'* the Holy Spirit (Acts 2:4; 4:8, 31; 9:17; 13:9, 52);
c) Sometimes he is said to be *'poured out'* on people (Acts 2:17, 18, 33; 10:45);
d) Sometimes people are said to *'receive'* the Holy Spirit (Acts 2:38; 8:15, 17, 19; 10:47; 19:2);
e) Sometimes he is said to *'be given'* to people (Acts 5:32; 8:18; 11:17; 15:8);
f) Sometimes he is said to *'fall upon'* people (Acts 8:16; 10:44; 11:15).

Baptism in the Holy Spirit, however, is a phrase which has a special ring about it. Whilst we can be 'filled' many times, we are 'baptised' in the Spirit' only once. That happens when we receive the power of the Spirit for the first time, and that occurs (as we will see later) when we are born again.

In building a kind of 'profile' of Spirit baptism we therefore have to begin with the realisation that baptism in the Holy Spirit is an essential feature of Christian initiation. Full initiation into the Kingdom of God involves four things: repentance of sin, believing in Jesus Christ, baptism in water, and baptism in the Holy Spirit (see Acts 2:38). If any one of these does not happen, then something must be done to rectify the situation as soon as possible.

It is in order to make this point that Luke tells two important stories in the Book of Acts. The first involves Philip in Acts 8. Philip preaches the gospel in a city in Samaria and many believe the Word and are baptised in water (8:12). It appears that they have fulfilled most of the requirements for initiation into the Kingdom of God: repentance, faith in Christ and water baptism. However, something is missing. Luke writes:

> *When the apostles in Jerusalem heard that Samaria had accepted the word of God, they sent Peter and John to them. When they arrived, they prayed for them that they might receive the Holy Spirit, because the Holy Spirit had not yet*

come upon any of them; they had simply been baptised into the name of the Lord Jesus. Then Peter and John placed their hands on them, and they received the Holy Spirit.

(Acts 8:14-17)

Why else does Luke tell this story if it is not to make the point that something is wrong if a new believer has not been immersed in the charismatic Spirit of God?

The same goes for the second story which Luke tells on this theme. In Acts 19, Paul arrives in Ephesus to find that there is a group of twelve disciples who have not received the gift of the Spirit. They had been baptised in water, but when that had happened it had not been in the name of Jesus. It had been a baptism for repentance, like John the Baptist's. So Luke reports what Paul did next:

On hearing this, they were baptised into the name of the Lord Jesus. When Paul placed his hands on them, the Holy Spirit came upon them, and they spoke in tongues and prophesied. There were about twelve men in all.

(Acts 19:5-7)

Again, why else does Luke tell this story if it is not to make the point that something essential was missing! viz., baptism in the Holy Spirit.

As far as our profile of Spirit baptism is concerned, we therefore need to begin by stressing that we are talking about the believer's initial reception of the Holy Spirit. When a person comes to faith and is born again, he receives the gift of the Holy Spirit. That experience of being filled for the first time is what John, Jesus, Peter and Paul meant by 'baptism in the Spirit'.

This means that baptism in the Spirit is an essential experience for every new believer. Whilst the normal Christian life involves us constantly being filled with the Holy Spirit (Ephesians 5:18), there is a first experience of being filled with the Spirit which the New Testament chooses to call 'being baptised in the Spirit'. It is my aim to try and explain something of this experience in this book.

16

3

Proof

From this profile we can see that the right time to pray for people to be baptised in the Holy Spirit is when they give their lives to Jesus Christ – in short, when they repent and believe for the very first time. In my experience, when we do this, new believers always experience the tangible anointing of the Holy Spirit. Various reactions are felt as the Spirit is poured into them. Various things also pour out of them as well!

When we lay hands on new believers and pray 'Come, Holy Spirit', what is the evidence or proof that they have been baptised in the Spirit? In what follows, we will look first of all at the 'internal proof' of baptism in the Spirit, and secondly at the 'external proof'. In short, we will look at what is technically known as 'initial evidence'.

a) Internal Proof

Spirit baptism has both a visible and an invisible dimension. The invisible dimension is the unseen invasion of the believer by the dynamic presence of the Spirit. When Luke says that all 120 disciples were 'filled' with the Holy Spirit (Acts 2:4), he is underlining the invisible and internal dimension of Spirit baptism.

It is important to understand that this internal filling was largely new in God's dealings with his people. Up until Pentecost, the anointing of the Holy Spirit was most commonly depicted as something which **came** *upon* select individuals. In the Greek translation of the Old Testament known as the Septuagint the anointing of the Spirit is usually depicted as something external. Thus the Spirit is often described as:

a.   *'falling upon'* (Ezekiel 11:5);

17

b.   *'coming upon'* (Ezekiel 2:2; 3:24);

c.   being *'placed upon'* (Numbers 11:17, 25);

d.   *'clothing'* (Judges 6:34; 1 Chronicles 12:18; 2 Chronicles 24:20);

e.   being *'given'* (Numbers 11:29; Nehemiah 9:20; Isaiah 42:1);

f.   *'resting upon'* (Judges 14:6, 19; 1 Samuel 10:6, 10; 11:6; 16:13);

h.   and *'appearing upon'* (Numbers 23:6; 24:2; Judges 3:10; 11:29; 1 Samuel 19:20, 23; 2 Kings 2:9; 2 Chronicles 15:1; 20:14).

With Pentecost, this changes. Now the Holy Spirit invades and fills all of God's people. The Spirit of God is now an internal, not just an external reality. No longer do the disciples have the Spirit. The Spirit has them!

This difference between an external anointing and an internal filling is very important, though we should not draw the line between them too thickly. The night before he died, Jesus said to his disciples:

> *'I will ask the Father, and he will give you another Counsellor, to be with you forever – the Spirit of truth. The world cannot accept him, because it neither sees him nor knows him. But you know him, for he lives with you **and will be in you'**.* (John 14:16-17)

Notice the wording in verse 17. Jesus says to the disciples that the Spirit of truth is **with** them. That is a present tense. Jesus is saying, 'During my ministry, the Holy Spirit has been with you' (*para humin*, in Greek). However, Jesus also promises that the same Spirit will soon be *in* them. That is a simple future. Jesus is saying, 'Shortly, the Holy Spirit will not longer just be **with** you but *in* you' (*en humin*, in Greek). Once Jesus is glorified (i.e. once he has returned to the Father), Jesus will give the disciples the Holy Spirit in such a way that the Spirit will be an internal reality, a power flowing from the believer's heart (John 7:37-38).

So baptism in the Holy Spirit has an internal dimension for the believer. When we are filled with the Spirit, a change takes place inside us. The Spirit fills us to the very depths of our being.

What kinds of experience do people have when they receive the gift of the Spirit for the very first time? The two basic responses are (as we would expect) repentance and faith. Repentance should be no surprise. It is one of the functions of the Holy Spirit to convict the world of sin (John 16:6-11). When we preach the Gospel and then ask the Holy Spirit to increase his presence upon the listeners, people will often be moved into a godly sorrow which leads to true repentance. Often this will be accompanied by weeping.

The second common response is faith. When the Spirit fills a person for the first time, he will suddenly believe in his heart that Jesus is risen (Romans 10:9), and that Jesus is Lord (1 Corinthians 12:3). Again, this is one of the primary functions of the Holy Spirit. The Spirit testifies in our hearts concerning the deity and the sovereignty of Jesus (John 16:14). To use the four titles which Pentecostals employ, the Spirit reveals to our hearts that Jesus is Saviour, Baptiser in the Spirit, Healer and Coming King (the Foursquare Gospel).

The fact is, when people open themselves up to receive the promised gift of the Spirit, the inner transformation which people then experience is profound. Repentance and faith flow into their hearts. Bondage is replaced by freedom. Death is replaced by life.

You see the point? Spirit baptism produces profound changes *on the inside*. Whilst there is no one stereotypical experience which happens to everyone, the fact is that being filled is an experience of the supernatural power of God. As people receive, they should feel something on the inside! They should not be treated like patients at a dentist's surgery and told, 'You won't feel a thing!'

b) External Proof

But baptism in the Spirit provides us with external as well as internal proof. When a believer is baptised in the Holy Spirit, there are outward signs of this invisible grace.

For Pentecostals, the outward proof is speaking in tongues. The grounds for this stem from five classic texts in Acts (the 'famous five', as it were). From these we can see instances in which people who are filled with the Spirit immediately exercise the spiritual gift of tongues. This happens to the disciples (Acts 2), to the Samaritans (Acts 8), to Paul (Acts 9), to Cornelius and his household (Acts 10), and to the Ephesian twelve (Acts 19). Clearly, speaking in unlearnt languages was evidence of Spirit baptism.

However, to say that tongues is the only outward evidence is really an over-simplification. It would be far more accurate to say that 'charismatic speech' is the main external evidence of Spirit baptism. By 'charismatic speech' I mean a variety of verbal expressions: praise, proclamation, and prophecy. These three phenomena are all examples of the main outward evidence of baptism with the Holy Spirit. Indeed, when a person is baptised in the Spirit, what pours out of their mouths is the best evidence of what has been poured into their hearts!

The scriptural support for this is the way in which Luke, both in his gospel and in his sequel (Acts), uses the phrase *'filled with the Spirit'*. There is a consistent pattern here and this has to do with 'inspired speaking'. On just about every occasion that Luke uses *'filled with the Spirit'*, it is followed by praise, proclamation or prophecy. Now obviously some of these texts refer to experiences of being filled after an initial reception of the Spirit (see Acts 4:31, for example). However, Luke's descriptions of people being Spirit-filled are important to our discussion because Luke uses *'filled with the Spirit'* when the 120 disciples are baptised in the Spirit at Pentecost (Acts 2:4). Clearly the consequences of being baptised in the Spirit and being filled with the Spirit are the same – even if the experiences themselves are different!

Let's look at some examples from Luke-Acts.

In Luke 1:41, Elizabeth (John the Baptist's mother) is *'filled with the Holy Spirit'* and 'inspired speech' is the immediate result:

When Elizabeth heard Mary's greeting, the baby leaped in

*her womb, and Elizabeth was **filled with the Holy Spirit**. In a loud voice she exclaimed, 'Blessed are you among women, and blessed is the child you will bear...'*

Here the result of being filled is prophecy. Elizabeth, inspired by the Spirit, cannot restrain herself from shouting out how blessed both Mary and her child are.

In Luke 1:67, it is the turn of Elizabeth's husband, Zechariah, to experience a similar work of God:

*His father Zechariah was **filled with the Holy Spirit** and prophesied: 'Praise be to the Lord, the God of Israel, because he has come and redeemed his people'.*

From vv. 69-75, Zechariah continues in this vein. His words are an inspired form of praise. But then, in vv. 76-79, he turns from looking upwards to God to looking down at his new baby. He turns from praise to prophecy:

'And you, my child, will be called a prophet of the Most High; for you will go on before the Lord to prepare the way for him...'

For Zechariah, then, being filled with the Holy Spirit produces two forms of charismatic speech: praise and prophecy.

In Acts, Luke repeats this pattern. In Acts 2:4, the immediate result of being filled is, for the 120 disciples, inspired speech:

*All of them were **filled with the Holy Spirit** and began to speak in other tongues as the Spirit enabled them.*

Here the 'charismatic speech' is praise, in the form of tongues.

But in Acts 4:8 it is anointed proclamation not tongues which follows the infilling of the Spirit:

*Then Peter, **filled with the Holy Spirit**, said to them, 'Rulers and elders of the people! If we are being called to account for an act of kindness shown to a cripple and are asked how*

21

he was healed, then know this, you and all the people of Israel: It is by the name of Jesus Christ of Nazareth, whom you crucified but whom God raised from the dead, that this man stands before you healed.'

Here bold preaching is the consequence of being Spirit-filled.

In Acts 4:31, we see a similar connection between being filled and preaching with power, effectiveness and courage. This time the story involves the believers who have been praising God for the release of Peter and John from prison:

*After they prayed, the place where they were meeting was shaken. And they were all **filled with the Holy Spirit** and spoke the word of God boldly.*

Here, 'inspired speech' is again the evidence. As in Acts 4:8, this inspired speech takes the form of anointed proclamation.

In Acts 13:9, Luke describes another kind of 'inspired speaking'. At this point Paul is in Cyprus, trying to preach the Gospel. However, a sorcerer named Elymas opposes him. This is what happens as Elymas follows Paul one day:

*Then Saul, who was also called Paul, **filled with the Holy Spirit**, looked straight at Elymas and said, 'You are a child of the devil and an enemy of everything that is right! You are full of all kinds of deceit and trickery. Will you never stop perverting the right ways of the Lord? Now the hand of the Lord is against you. You are going to be blind, and for a time you will be unable to see the light of the sun'.*

In this instance, the kind of 'inspired speech' which Paul uses is clearly prophecy. He exercises the gift of discernment in seeing what is motivating Elymas. He then operates in the gift of prophecy as he warns Elymas what will befall him. Here, being filled with the Spirit produces prophecy rather than praise or proclamation.

The point I am making is that there is external proof of baptism in the Holy Spirit. When we look at the occasions in Luke and

Acts when people are *'filled with the Holy Spirit'*, what we find is a consistent pattern. People, when they are filled, start uttering 'charismatic speech'. They are enabled for inspired speaking. This speech can take a number of forms, from praise to prophecy to proclamation. We will spend a few more paragraphs looking at each of these.

First of all, praise. When a person is baptised in the Holy Spirit, he suddenly discovers joy in worship. C.S. Lewis' autobiography was called 'Surprised by Joy' and this is a perfect description of one result of Spirit baptism. Sadly, many Christians only start to experience this beautiful side-effect a long time after their initial reception of the Spirit at conversion. Recently an elderly Christian man came up to me at a cricket match and asked if he could sit and talk to me. He sat down and started to speak:

> I have been a committed evangelical Christian all my life. I have had my quiet times, prayed, done as much witnessing as I could, gone to church, tithed, everything. But in it all, something was missing. Then, a few months ago, I was anointed by the Holy Spirit and, do you know what, now I can't stop crying. Every time I find myself in a context of worship, I can't stop weeping for joy. It's as if years of godly emotions have suddenly been set free and I can at last praise the Lord with total freedom.

If you were to ask me what evidence I look for when praying for someone to receive the Holy Spirit at conversion, enthusiastic praise and rejoicing is one of the signs. After all, the Bible says *'The Lord inhabits the praises of his people'*, not 'The Lord *inhibits* the praises of his people!'

A second piece of evidence is proclamation. By 'proclamation' I mean an inspired boldness in sharing the Gospel with others. When the disciples were baptised in the Holy Spirit, Peter was empowered for anointed preaching. He was given a holy boldness in communicating the message of salvation to those who witnessed the Pentecost event. He was passionate about his subject, he was direct in his challenge, he was fearless in his approach. He was enabled to quote just the right Scriptures in just the right way (Act 2:17-21, 25-28, 34-35). He was given great confidence in his presentation (Acts 2:29). He was equipped with persuasive arguments for convincing his hearers about the resurrection (Acts 2:30-32). In short, he was anointed with the rhetoric of the Spirit.

It is my experience that a person who is baptised in the Holy Spirit is empowered for mission. God starts to engineer divine appointments – meetings with just the right people at just the right time. Moreover, he gives a tremendous confidence in the Gospel and a remarkable ability to say just the right words.

Look at this letter which I received several days after praying for a couple to receive the Holy Spirit. Three of us prayed for both of them for an evening and the results were immediate. Margaret, the wife, wrote:

> I feel that I must write and thank you and your friends for your helpful ministry to Peter and myself on Tuesday. I am still basking in the afterglow! I shall never forget the experience of God's power and the way you worked in such harmony to allow it to happen. Since then I have felt cleansed through my whole being and also great joy, despite our present difficult circumstances. Only the Lord could do this, for which I give him thanks and praise.
>
> I have already been able to share some of my experiences with my sister, friends and workmates. This morning, quite out of the blue, a Drugs Rep. working at the surgery asked me if I believed in the supernatural and I was able to share with her some of the things the Lord had shown me on Tuesday night. I know God gave me this opportunity and that there will be many more…

A boldness in sharing the faith and a passion for the lost is one proof of a person's Spirit baptism. How right Pentecostals are to emphasise that baptism in the Holy Spirit involves 'empowerment for mission'. When a person receives the power of the Spirit, anointed evangelism starts to happen. Signs start to follow the preaching of the Gospel. Indeed, we start to live in the truth of Hebrews 2 verse 4:

God also testified to it (the message of salvation) by signs, wonders and various miracles, and gifts of the Holy Spirit distributed according to his will.

A third proof is prophecy. When the 120 disciples were baptised in the Holy Spirit at Pentecost, Peter stood up and said that what was happening was in fulfilment of a prophecy uttered by Joel. Part of Joel's prophecy was itself a promise concerning prophecy! It reads:

'In the last days', God says, 'I will pour out my Spirit on all people. Your sons and daughters will prophesy, your young men will see visions, your old men will dream dreams. Even on my servants, both men and women, I will pour out my Spirit in those days, and they will prophesy!' (Acts 2:17-18)

The importance of this Scripture should not be missed. In the Old Testament, only a select few were anointed to be prophets. Moses, however, wished that all God's people could prophesy (Numbers 11:29). That great day arrived at Pentecost. When the Spirit fell upon the disciples in Jerusalem, they were all anointed for prophecy. No one was left out. Both young and old, male and female, all were enabled to prophesy.

What, then, is prophecy? We should not drive too hard a wedge between prophecy and proclamation, for prophecy is also bold, inspired speech. It is the verbal communication of a vision, dream, picture, message or Scripture which has been divinely revealed by the Spirit. Its origin is in the mind of Christ, its destination is the church, its vehicle is the Spirit, and its purpose is edification (1 Corinthians 14:3). Every church needs prophecy!

Prophecy is an important form of inspired speech. It is a gift which is given to those who are baptised in the Holy Spirit. It is **a** gift of the Spirit which follows **the** gift of the Spirit! Those who minister to candidates wanting to receive the baptism in the Holy Spirit should ask the candidate to report any dreams, visions, pictures, messages or Scriptures which impact them over subsequent weeks or months. Sooner or later the candidate may well start to operate in this gift.

In conclusion: when a person is baptised in the Holy Spirit, a number of things happen. Internally he experiences a profound awakening, liberation and transformation. These stem from the repentance and faith which the Holy Spirit produces inside our hearts.

Externally, he starts to praise, to prophesy, and to proclaim the Good News. 'Inspired speaking' becomes part of his daily life in the Spirit. Such a man simply cannot stop praising God, speaking out Scripture, praying with fervour, uttering revelatory pictures or words, and – most importantly – gossiping the Gospel!

4

Purpose

It is now time to turn our attention to the purpose of baptism in the Spirit. We have seen so far that it is an essential part of our initiation ('the normal Christian birth'), that it is a profound experience, and that there is always evidence of its reality in a new believer's life. Why, then, does God want us to be baptised in the Holy Spirit? What, in brief, is its purpose?

It is at this point that we need to look in some depth at Jesus' experience of Spirit baptism at the River Jordan. In many ways Mark, Matthew and Luke present this event as a kind of model for the disciple's initial reception of the Spirit. We can therefore learn a great deal from the Master's example. Indeed, we will soon see that the purposes for which the Lord was baptised in the Holy Spirit are similar for us today.

Over the next few pages we will examine Mark's account of the Jordan experience. His is the shortest version, and it is the most convenient for our discussion of the purpose of Spirit baptism:

> *At that time Jesus came from Nazareth in Galilee and was baptised by John in the Jordan. As Jesus was coming up out of the water, he saw heaven being torn open and the Spirit descending on him like a dove. And a voice came from heaven: 'You are my Son, whom I love; with you I am well pleased.'* (Mark 1:9-11)

From this brief passage, and also from its context in Mark's Gospel, I would like to suggest that the Spirit baptism of Jesus had three specific purposes. These three purposes can be summed up under the headings, 'sonship', 'service' and 'sacrifice'. We will examine all three of these purposes in relation to Jesus, and then in relation to ourselves.

a. Sonship

Let us begin by noticing who is involved in the baptism of Jesus in the River Jordan. At the human level, only two people are mentioned, John the Baptist and of course Jesus of Nazareth. At the divine level, however, there are three persons at work in this event. There is the Son who is baptised. There is the Spirit who descends upon him. There is the Father who declares his pleasure. At the divine level, the baptism of Jesus is an event involving the Father, the Son and the Holy Spirit. It is an action involving all three persons of the Holy Trinity.

The first thing to say about Jesus' Spirit baptism is therefore this: that it contained a profound revelation of Jesus' sonship and a profound revelation of the Father's love. When the Spirit baptises Jesus, the heavens are torn open and Jesus hears the Father shouting out in both heaven and on earth, 'You are my Son, whom I love; with you I am well pleased'. Jesus hears the Father saying, 'I love you, my Son'.

It is difficult to know quite how conscious Jesus was of his unique sonship **before** this event. I suspect that this knowledge grew as he grew. We can be sure of one thing, however. After his baptism, Jesus can have been in no doubt at all about this eternal sonship. He would have known with complete and unshakeable certainty that he was the unique Son of God. He would have known that God is 'Abba', 'Dear Father', and that he was destined for a very special task.

b. Service

If Jesus' baptism in the Spirit involved a powerful affirmation of his sonship, it also involved a tremendous experience of power for service and for mission. When the Spirit came down upon Jesus, he was immersed in the supernatural power of God as surely as he had just been immersed in the waters of Jordan. He was anointed for charismatic ministry in a way that he had not been before.

It is extremely important at this point to read the story of Jesus' baptism in its immediate context. We will first of all see that just before his baptism, Jesus is referred to by John the Baptist as *'a More Powerful One'*. John says, *'After me will come a More Powerful One than I'* (Mark 1:7). Immediately after that, Jesus appears and receives power from heaven at his baptism. Immediately after **that**, Jesus begins a ministry of power and authority. He preaches about the Kingdom of God and wins disciples (Mark 1:14-20). He teaches with an authority that astonishes his listeners (1:21-22). He delivers those who are demonised (1:23-28). He heals many sick people (1:29-34). As Mark puts it,

> *'He travelled throughout Galilee, preaching in the synagogues, and driving out demons.'* (Mark 1:39)

Clearly, then, Jesus' baptism in the Spirit was a special empowerment for Kingdom service and mission. He is empowered for a charismatic ministry of healing the sick, preaching the Good News, and binding Satan in all of his manifestations (which includes the Pharisees who literally 'tempt' him, Mark 8:11). For Jesus, baptism in the Holy Spirit was therefore an anointing with power for the battle against Satan's limited kingdom. That is why the verse after the baptism story says:

> *At once the Spirit sent him out into the desert, and he was in the desert for forty days, being tempted by Satan.*

c. Sacrifice

This anointing was not for a life of invincibility. It was not an anointing to become an invulnerable Superman. There are indications throughout his Gospel that Mark thought of this Spirit baptism as an anointing for sacrificial servanthood. In other words, there is good evidence that Mark saw this Spirit baptism as God's way of equipping his Son with the necessary resources for giving his life as a ransom for many (Mark 10:45). At this point it is important to read the story of Jesus' baptism in the overall context of Mark's gospel.

Notice one unique feature of Mark's account of Jesus' baptism. In Mark we read that the heavens were 'torn open'. In Matthew and Luke, we read that the heavens were merely 'opened'. The difference between Mark's 'torn open' and Matthew and Luke's 'opened' is very dramatic. In Greek, 'torn open' comes from the verb *schizein* (from which we get the word 'schism'), while 'opened' comes from the verb *anoigein*. Why does Mark *schizein* when the others use *anoigein*?

The answer lies in the story of Jesus' death in Mark 15. The next time anything will be 'torn open' in Mark's gospel is in Mark 15:38-39, where we read of two very significant effects of the death of Jesus. The first involves the Jewish Temple, and the second involves the Roman centurion:

> *The curtain of the Temple was torn in two from top to bottom. And when the centurion, who stood there in front of Jesus, heard his cry and saw how he died, he said 'Surely this man was the Son of God!'*

As Jesus dies, the first thing that happens is that the Temple curtain is torn open. The Greek verb for 'torn open' is *schizein*, the same word that was used for the heavens being 'torn open' at Jesus' baptism. The second thing that happens is that the centurion at the cross proclaims Jesus as 'the Son of God'. This is the same kind of revelation which occurs after the heavens are torn open at Jesus' baptism. There the Father also declares that Jesus is his Son. So Mark (whom many wrongly think of as a poor storyteller) has very cleverly set up a rich parallel between the baptism of Jesus and the death of Jesus. We may put it thus:

At the baptism of Jesus, the heavens are torn open and the Father declares that Jesus is his Son. At the death of Jesus, the curtain is torn open and the centurion proclaims that Jesus is God's Son!

The purpose behind this can only be that Mark sees Jesus'

baptism in the Spirit not only as an anointing to do with sonship and service, but an anointing which is also to do with sacrifice. The baptism with which Jesus is baptised (see Mark 10:39) is an anointing for martyrdom as well as for miracles. It is an empowerment for fidelity unto death.

So there seems to be at least a threefold purpose for Jesus' baptism in the Holy Spirit. It was for sonship, for service, and for sacrifice. Let us now apply these three purposes to our own experience of baptism in the Holy Spirit.

a. Sonship

When a person is baptised in the Holy Spirit today, one of the invariable consequences is that Galatians 4:6 becomes a reality in his heart. In this passage, Paul writes:

> *Because you are sons, God sent the Spirit of his Son into our hearts, the Spirit who calls out, '**Abba**, Father'.*

There is a very similar passage in Romans 8:15-16. There Paul writes:

> *For you did not receive a spirit that makes you a slave again to fear, but you received the Spirit of adoption. And by him we cry, '**Abba**, Father'. The Spirit himself testifies with our spirit that we are God's children.*

In my experience, when someone is baptised in the Spirit, they almost always come into a profound awareness of the Father's special love for them. Just as Jesus, at his baptism, heard the Father shout from heaven, 'That's my Son, the Son whom I love!', so people today receive a very deep and strong impression of the truth of those words in John 16:27:

> *'The Father himself loves you...'*

Take the following testimony as an example. This is the

31

experience of a friend of mine:

> I was brought up by a father who adored my sister but who
> ignored me. He used to say that I was not even his child.
> That someone else was the father. In my forties I gave my
> life to Jesus Christ and went to two Spirit-filled friends to
> ask them to pray for me. As they did, the Holy Spirit came
> upon me in such a powerful way that I had to kneel down on
> the floor. Then the man (who knew nothing of my past), had
> a word of knowledge: 'You have a father who thinks that
> you are not his child. But your Heavenly Father wants you to
> know that you are his child, and that he loves you dearly'.
> As you can imagine, these words had a profound effect on
> my life. For the first time I could relate to God as Father! I
> was filled with a deep sense of assurance about my worth in
> the Father's eyes.

Stories like this are very typical. I hear them all the time. They
are stories of people whose experience of baptism in the Holy
Spirit is an experience of sonship. They now know in their hearts
that the Father himself loves them, and moreover they are able to
cry out to God, '**Abba**, dear Father!' They are now able to
worship God with the intimate adoration of a little child.

b. Service

Another purpose for baptism in the Holy Spirit can be summed up
in the phrase, 'empowerment for service'. One reason why God
wants to give his Holy Spirit to new believers is because from that
moment on they can experience God's *dunamis*, the Greek word
translated as 'power'. This power is vital for effective service.

As most Christians know, *dunamis* is the word from which we
get 'dynamite'. When we experience baptism in the Holy Spirit,
we become aware of the awesome dynamite of God! We become
acutely conscious that there is, at work in our lives, what Paul
described as a power *'which is like the working of God's mighty
strength, which he exerted in Christ when he raised him from the*

dead' (Ephesians 1:19-20). We start to experience that charismatic energy which transformed Christ's corpse into a resurrection body. In short, we start to operate in the power of the resurrection!

From the moment of Spirit baptism it therefore becomes possible to do the works of Jesus today. Jesus' works consisted of many things, and noticeable amongst these were *dunameis* or 'mighty deeds'. In Jesus, *dunamis* (power) produced *dunameis* (acts of power). These 'mighty works' consisted of authoritative preaching and wonderworking signs, particularly healing and exorcism. From the Jordan experience onwards, Jesus became 'mighty in word and deed'. He manifested the Kingdom of God in both words and works.

When we are baptised in the Holy Spirit, we therefore receive power to be effective witnesses for Jesus (Acts 1:8). Baptism in the Spirit equips us with a kind of charismatic PhD! In other words, we are anointed for

P – reaching
H – ealing
D – eliverance.

Needless to say, all of us are supposed to have PhDs. The normal Christian life is charismatic! We are all supposed to know God's *'incomparably great power for us who believe'* (Ephesians 1:19).

Sadly, many Christians do not operate in this power from the moment of their conversion – for reasons which we will discuss in the next chapter. Sometimes it is only years after their initial reception of the Spirit that many start to appreciate the power of the Spirit.

Take D.L. Moody as an example. He was a highly respected preacher of the gospel for years before, in 1871, he was confronted by two women who told him they were praying for him to receive 'spiritual power'. This happened for a while before Moody had a profound experience of the Spirit which W.R. Moody described as follows:

I thought I had power. I had the largest congregation in

33

Chicago, and there were many conversions. I was in a sense satisfied. But these two godly women kept praying for me and their earnest talk about anointing for special service set me thinking. There came a great hunger into my soul. I did not know what it was. I began to cry out as I never did before. I really felt that I did not want to live if I could not have this power for service.

I was crying all the time that God would fill me with His Spirit. Well, one day, in the city of New York – oh, what a day! – I cannot describe it, I seldom refer to it; it is almost too sacred an experience to name. I can only say that God revealed himself to me, and I had to ask Him to stay His hand. I went to preaching again. The sermons were not different; I did not present any new truths; and yet hundreds were converted. I would not now be placed back where I was before that blessed experience if you should give me all the world – it would be as the small dust of the balance.

What a wonderful description of the experience of being 'filled with the Holy Spirit'! Is this not a release of 'power for service', as Moody himself says? How impoverished we are if we fail to tap into the immensely powerful resources given to us by the Spirit at our conversion!

c. Sacrifice

A word of warning, however. For Jesus, baptism in the Holy Spirit was not just an empowerment for service, it was an empowerment for sacrifice. The same will be true for those who are baptised in the Holy Spirit today. Being drenched in the *dunamis* of God will enable us to experience the power of Easter Day, but it will also involve us in the pain of Good Friday. Paul knew this. That is why he said, *'I want to know Christ and the power of his resurrection and the fellowship of sharing in his sufferings, becoming like him in his death'* (Philippians 3:10). Paul knew that the true Christian is baptised into a lifestyle of costly discipleship as well as charismatic power.

I hope the reader will forgive me if I do not develop this vital point. This is because I am currently writing a book for Sovereign World entitled, *Work of the Cross, Work of the Spirit*, and I do not want to pre-empt what I shall say there. What I will say is this: that the blessings of Spirit baptism are not for us to lead comfortable lives but are for sacrificial service. The blessing, in short, is for the battle. That is why Jesus, immediately after being baptised in the Spirit, finds himself in the desert engaged in costly warfare with Satan (Mark 1:12). Spirit baptism did not lead to a path of shallow triumphalism but rather to what the poet T.S. Eliot called 'a condition of complete simplicity, costing not less than everything' *(The Four Quartets).*

Something of this third purpose of Spirit baptism is captured in the lovely testimony of Antoinette Moomean of Eustice, Nebraska, who left the Mission field in China to find out what was going on at the Asuza Street Revival. She duly experienced a fresh touch of the Holy Spirit in power. In the *Apostolic Faith* (1908) she wrote as follows:

> The Lord showed me that the cross was going to mean to me what it had never meant before. One morning the Spirit dealt with me, singing through me –
>
> > Must Jesus bear the cross alone,
> > And all the world go free?
> > No, there's a cross for everyone,
> > And there is one for me.
>
> The last line He seemed to burn into my soul by repeating it over and over again. Sometimes the Spirit would sing a line and then sob out a line. Although I wept and was in anguish of soul, it was all in the Spirit.

What a super example of this third purpose of baptism in the Spirit! Far from being anointed for an invincible ministry, Antoinette Moomean recognised what many have failed to see – that the fullness is for the fight! Indeed, later in the same testimony, she speaks of how the experience of baptism in the Spirit

> ...gave me to understand the secret of the endurance of the martyrs who were burned at the stake with the glory of heaven upon their faces, and seemingly free from pain.

What was true for Antoinette will be true for those of us who seek the fullness of the Spirit's power. Life will not become easier. However, we will have the immense resources of the Spirit with which to confront the dark clouds of spiritual battle. With those, we can be 'strong in the Lord and in the power of his might!' We can learn to operate with 'the endurance of the martyrs!'

5

Problems

Before we go any further, we must now look at a major problem associated with our subject. This problem really revolves around the timing of Spirit baptism. In other words, Christians who talk about Spirit baptism often disagree about when it happens exactly. Broadly speaking, there are three views: the first says that we are baptised in the Spirit when we are baptised in water (the sacramental view). The second says that we are baptised in the Spirit after we are converted, at a later date (the Pentecostal view). The third says that we are baptised in the Spirit when we are converted (the evangelical view). We will look at these three views in more detail now.

a. The Sacramental View

This view sees baptism in the Holy Spirit as something which occurs during the sacrament of water baptism. As the candidate is immersed in the waters of baptism, so he is immersed in the power of God's Holy Spirit. Put very simplistically, in the **sacramental** perspective, water baptism and Spirit baptism happen at one and the same time.

Of course, the real difficulty with this is that both the New Testament and our own Christian experience do not seem to bear it out. I know of no Christian friend who regards their baptism in water, either as an infant or as an adult, as the occasion for the kinds of experience which I have described in this book. In some cases, baptism in the Spirit has occurred prior to water baptism. In other cases, baptism in the Spirit occurs after water baptism. I have not yet met anyone who really experienced both simultaneously, though there may be many who have.

Furthermore, it is worthwhile noting that even in the case of

Jesus' baptism at Jordan, the Spirit descends on Jesus **after** he has come up from the water. In Luke's gospel, the gap of time between this ascent from the water and this descent of the Spirit is emphasised. Luke's account reads as follows:

> *When all the people were being baptised, Jesus was baptised too. And as he was praying, heaven was opened and the Holy Spirit descended on him in bodily form.*
>
> (Luke 3:21-22)

According to Luke, Jesus' reception of the Spirit occurred after his baptism and during a period of prayer! It did not occur immediately he came out of the water. Luke does not seem to see a necessary link between water baptism and Spirit baptism.

Luke continues to make this point in the Book of Acts. Here there is no uniform pattern concerning the relationship between water baptism and Spirit baptism. When the 120 disciples are baptised in the Spirit on the day of Pentecost there is no sign of any water baptism at all! (Acts 2:1-4). When the Ethiopian eunuch is baptised in water, there is no sign of any Spirit baptism at all! (Acts 8:26-40). When Saul is converted, he is baptised in the Holy Spirit **before** he is baptised in water (Acts 9:17-18). The same goes for Cornelius and his household in Acts 10:47-48. However, the Samaritan converts are baptised in water before they are baptised in the Spirit (Acts 8:16-17), and the same goes for the Ephesian disciples in Acts 19:5-6.

As far as the sacramental view is concerned, the evidence of Scripture and experience would suggest that it is unwise to be too dogmatic. Water baptism and Spirit baptism do not always seem to occur at the same time.

b. The Pentecostal View

Perhaps the most popular view today is the Pentecostal view. At the heart of Pentecostalism is the belief that there are two distinct blessings which God wants to give us. The first is called regeneration, or being 'born again'. This consists of repentance, faith and water baptism but it does not include receiving the gift of the Spirit. That occurs at a subsequent date, when a person is baptised in the Holy Spirit. When that happens, the Spirit fills the believer, empowering him for mission in the world. It is at this second stage that the Spirit is received. Until we have experienced this second blessing, we can (say many Pentecostals) believe in Christ without having received the Spirit. Perhaps the clearest statement of this 'theology of subsequence' is in Don Basham's famous booklet, *A Handbook on Holy Spirit Baptism*. Here he speaks of two separate experiences:

> The first is conversion; the sinner's acceptance of Jesus Christ as Lord and Saviour which brings salvation. He (the repentant sinner) gives testimony to his response to the gospel and his acceptance of Christ by receiving baptism in water for the remission of sins. Here we see the new believer as the **object** of God's redemption. But the Lord is not satisfied with our conversion alone; He has promised us power to be His witnesses. So, a second time we are confronted with the power of God, this time in the baptism with the Holy Spirit through which the Christian is brought into a deeper relationship with Christ and the Holy Spirit for the purpose of making him – not an **object** – but an **instrument** of redemption.

What are we to make of this two-stage view? On the surface it sounds plausible. In John 3:5, Jesus himself seems to teach about two blessings when he speaks of the importance of being born of water (which Pentecostals equate with regeneration), and being born of the Spirit (which they equate with Spirit baptism). Pentecostals also point to the two principal ministries of Jesus as indicated by John the Baptist in John 1:29-34: he is the Lamb of God who removes our sins and the Messiah who baptises us in the Holy Spirit. This, they argue, confirms that there are two stages for us to undergo in the Christian life. Pentecostals also argue from Acts that the Samaritans are given two blessings, one consisting of repentance, faith and water baptism (Acts 8:12), the other consisting of baptism in the Holy Spirit (Acts 8:17). Similar claims are made for the Ephesian Twelve at the beginning of Acts 19.

However, as in the case of the sacramental view, things are not as 'water-tight' as they seem. For example, the conversion of Cornelius in Acts 10 seems to go right against this Pentecostal view of two separate blessings. In Acts 10:44, we read that the Holy Spirit drenched Cornelius and his household even as Peter was preaching! Peter's sermon was interrupted by a demonstration of the Spirit's power in which the listeners were baptised in the Spirit. They received the gift of the Spirit and started speaking in tongues and praising God (Acts 10:46).

No amount of clever theological argument can remove the difficulties here. The problem for Pentecostals is that Cornelius and his household seem to have both blessings rolled into one! There is no talk of a first experience of regeneration (marked by repentance, faith and water baptism). Cornelius and his household are only said to receive what Pentecostals call the 'second blessing'. In other words, they go straight to baptism in the Holy Spirit and this is regarded by the apostolic community as sufficient evidence of their full conversion.

The main problem with the Pentecostal view is that it fails to account for the work of the Spirit in what it calls the first blessing. This first blessing consists of repentance, faith and water baptism, and Pentecostals argue that these occur without us receiving the gift of the Spirit. However, I have already shown that the New Testament as a whole does not agree with this. The Holy Spirit convicts us of sin and produces repentance in our lives. The Holy Spirit works in our lives in such a way that we can believe and confess Jesus as Lord! In other words, we must receive the Spirit during what Pentecostals refer to as the first blessing, during regeneration and conversion. I want humbly to suggest, therefore, that it is not possible to argue that 'salvation precedes baptism in the Spirit, or, to put it a bit differently, that one may truly believe in Christ and not yet have received the gift of the Holy Spirit' (Rodman Williams).

Talk of a second blessing (defined as baptism in the Holy Spirit) is therefore problematic. Things are not as simple as they appear in the Pentecostal perspective.

c. The Evangelical View

The third position is the evangelical view of Spirit baptism. All evangelicals argue that people receive the Spirit when they become Christians. This is because Paul says that *'if anyone does not have the Spirit of Christ, he does not belong to Christ'* (Romans 8:9). So as soon as a person belong to Christ, he must have the Spirit of Christ! Conversion marks the moment when we receive the Spirit. Being born again and being baptised in the Spirit are not to be separated. Indeed, the evangelical will want to say, *'What God has joined together, let not man divide!'*

The clearest statement of this position is to be found in John Stott's excellent little book, *Baptism and Fulness*, subtitled 'The Work of the Holy Spirit Today'. On page 26, the author confirms this view that conversion marks the moment of Spirit baptism. He writes:

> When sinners repent and believe, Jesus not only takes away their sins but also baptises them with his Spirit.

The point is underlined on page 36, when we read that

> ...the gift of the Holy Spirit is a **universal** Christian experience because it is an **initial** Christian experience. All Christians receive the Holy Spirit at the very beginning of their Christian life.

Speaking personally, I do not see how any Christian who is familiar with the Scriptures can possibly disagree with John Stott's position. The overall teaching of the Bible makes it clear that baptism in the Holy Spirit is our initial reception of the gift of the Spirit, and that this initial reception occurs at conversion. Indeed, it is impossible to deny this when Paul makes it so abundantly plain that no one can declare that Jesus is Lord except by the Holy Spirit.

Does this mean that the evangelical understanding of baptism in the Spirit is correct? The answer to that is, 'Yes... as far as it goes!' Evangelicals are right to stress that Spirit baptism is initiatory in character. The very choice of the word 'baptism' proves the point, for baptism is a rite of initiation. But the significance of the verb 'baptise' does not end here. The verb, as I showed in chapter two, was used of garments which were totally immersed in dye. This same word was then chosen by John, Jesus, Peter and Paul to denote the new believer's reception of the Spirit. This was because the initial reception of the Spirit by first century Christians was an overwhelming, supernatural experience.

Now it is precisely at this point that evangelicals stop short. They quite rightly point out that the word 'baptise' proves that Spirit baptism must be initiatory in character. But they fail to go on to point out that the same word was also chosen to describe an actual experience – an experience of being totally filled with the Spirit. In other words, they emphasise initiation but neglect immersion. The result is that they do not encourage new converts to experience immersion in the Spirit. Converts are simply told after the event that saying the 'sinner's prayer' and 'coming to Christ' was, for them, 'baptism in the Holy Spirit'. The fact that the vast majority of them had no vivid sense of encountering the Spirit is regarded as unimportant. Feelings, many will tell you, are dangerous.

The major problem with the evangelical view is therefore this: that is separates doctrine and experience. It rightly says that baptism in the Spirit occurs at conversion, but it wrongly neglects the actual experience of that event. Indeed, there is a real suspicion of experience of the Spirit amongst many evangelical Christians today. Many regard such things as emotional (which of course they are!). For those who really feel this way, I can only offer the following wise words of David Watson's in both humility and love:

> How can you have a vital relationship with the Living Lord Jesus without some experience? How can you be filled with the mighty Spirit of God without some experience? How can you worship God in Spirit and truth without some experience? Certainly we must be aware of seeking experiences just for their own sake, but the New Testament portrait of the Christian is full of superlatives: the peace

which passes understanding, the love which surpasses knowledge, unutterable and exalted joy.

(One in the Spirit, p.69)

d. A Conciliatory View

So there are problems associated with our subject, 'Baptism in the Holy Spirit', and these problems relate to timing. What, then, is the solution? After a good deal of reflection, prayer, discussion and study, I have come to the conclusion that the best solution to the current confusion is a combination of the most biblical aspects of all three views so far mentioned.

My strong conviction is that the evangelical position is right: baptism in the Spirit is part of our initiation into the Kingdom of God; it occurs when we truly repent of sin and confess Jesus as Lord for the very first time.

The sacramental view is therefore also close to the truth. Spirit baptism and water baptism should both be aspects of our conversion-initiation. They are not supposed to be separated in time.

What, then, of the Pentecostal view? Whilst disagreeing with the notion of Spirit baptism as a second blessing, I will agree with one thing: baptism in the Spirit is a charismatic experience of being filled, immersed and empowered in a tangible way by the supernatural reality of God. Pentecostals are absolutely right to insist on this.

Combining the best aspects of the three positions I would therefore say the following: according to the Scriptures, baptism in the Holy Spirit is a crucial part of our initiation into the Christian faith; that ideally it should occur as near as possible to our water baptism; and that it is a profound **experience** of the Spirit of God. Indeed, I would wholeheartedly agree with Professor Jimmy Dunn, who writes in his book *Baptism in the Holy Spirit* (p.4) that:

> The high point in conversion-initiation is the gift of the Spirit, and the beginning of the Christian life is to be reckoned from the experience of Spirit baptism.

43

That seems to me well said, but saying it, we are left with an important pastoral and theological question. Why is it that so many people only experience the power of the Spirit in a dramatic way at a date subsequent to their conversion? Why is it that so many actually feel immersed much later, and then mistakenly view that experience as 'baptism in the Holy Spirit'? Let me offer four possible reasons which are particularly true for Christians in the West:

a. Defective Doctrine
Many Christians teach – or at least imply – that supernatural experiences of the Spirit were for the apostolic age but are not for today. Such people usually accept the defective doctrine known as 'cessationism', which originated with St. Augustine and was elaborated by B.B. Warfield. Cessationism basically asserts that supernatural Christianity ceased at the end of the first century AD and that it is not for today. However, there is absolutely no evidence whatsoever in Scripture for this position (see John Ruthven's book, *On the Cessation of the Charismata* – Sheffield: Sheffield Academic Press, 1993). The fact is, there are no doctrinal reasons for neglecting or denying the profound experience of the Spirit in our lives today. When a person repents of sin and confesses Jesus as Lord, he should be taught about receiving the supernatural and dynamic gift which the Father has promised to all who call upon his name. He should be encouraged to open his heart and receive the Spirit, and to receive in whatever way the Spirit sovereignly determines.

b. Enlightenment Prejudice
The point has been made many times in recent years that the church in the West has, over the past few centuries, bought into the philosophical world-view of its culture. That world-view is the one forged during the Enlightenment or 'The Age of Reason'. It is a world-view which has no room for the supernatural, for the miraculous, for revelation.

One reason why most Christians do not experience the Spirit at conversion is because they have unconsciously agreed with the world-view that is anti-supernatural. This creates immense problems as far as Spirit baptism is concerned. The Holy Spirit is a supernatural reality. The spiritual gifts are supernatural endowments. Those Christians who buy into a world-view that worships 'Reason' will almost invariably fail to experience the touch of the Spirit at their conversion. A lack of expectation on their part, and very likely on the part of those who lead them to Christ, will cause a delay in their experience of the gift of the Spirit.

c. Psychological Resistance

In my experience, one of the commonest causes of the delay of this experience is quite simply fear, particularly a fear of losing control. We live in a culture where we have learnt over many years the art of keeping control. We have learnt to keep control over our lives (the curse of self-sufficiency) and we have learnt to keep control over our emotions (the curse of repression). I can well remember the first time I was exposed to an environment in which the Holy Spirit was very obviously at work. People were crying, laughing, falling over, speaking in tongues, shouting, singing, being healed, prophesying, dancing and generally behaving as if they were drunk (see Acts 2:13!). Inside I felt two emotions: a deep-seated anxiety and fear that this might happen to me, and an equally deep-seated longing that God would not exclude me from the blessing!

A fear of losing control is a very common cause of delay when it comes to experiencing the Spirit in power. The fact is, when the Spirit comes, we **do** lose control. Control is given over to the sovereign Spirit of God! It is no longer we who call the shots but him! We have to learn to enjoy his spontaneous work in our hearts. We have to learn to celebrate his sudden interruptions of our church services! If we are emotionally resistant to this kind of thing, no wonder it sometimes takes a long time for us to thaw out and warm up to the idea of being completely on fire in the Spirit!

d. Emotional Damage

Another common reason for a delay in experiencing the gift of the Spirit is unhealedness. I am particularly referring here to what I call 'father hunger'; in other words, to the trauma of not having a

45

father in childhood. I was born an illegitimate child, the son of a single parent mother, and immediately put in an orphanage with my twin sister. I have therefore never known my natural, true father. One reason why I believe I (and many others too) experienced a delay before knowing the fullness of the Spirit was because I simply could not face intimacy with my Heavenly Father. It is, after all, one of the functions of the Spirit to release a person into crying out to God, **Abba!** Dear Father! It liberates a person into sonship. For a long while I simply found this too painful, and so my Christianity remained Jesus-centred.

The turning point came when I realised that God had adopted me and me his child, and most importantly that he would never leave me:

> Father God, I wonder
> how I managed to exist
> without the knowledge of your parenthood
> and your loving care;
> but now I am your child
> I am adopted in your family
> and I can never be alone
> 'cos Father God you're there beside me!

Singing that song of Ishmael's for the first time was the moment when I began to be healed of my 'father hunger'. It also helped to release me in the gift of tongues. In some mysterious way, being able to cry out **Abba!** to God was vital for this particular spiritual gift. I did not know why until quite recently, when I uttered publicly the tongue which I use in private prayer. A woman translated it as follows:

> You are my Father. You pour out your blessings upon me like silver rain and I love you. I love you with all of my heart, my dearest Papa.

Perhaps one reason why so many of us experience a delay in experiencing the fullness of the Spirit is because there is so much unhealed 'father hunger' in us. If baptism in the Spirit releases us

46

into adopted sonship, is that any surprise?

Concluding Remarks

These, then, are just some of the causes of delay in actually experiencing the Spirit: defective doctrine, enlightenment prejudice, psychological resistance and emotional damage. In each of these and other ways, the devil robs God's people of a blessing which is their rightful inheritance. That blessing we may describe as 'the experience of the gift given at conversion, the gift of the Spirit'. In these four ways (and others too), we are denied a vital aspect of the normal Christian birth, namely the experience of the charismatic presence and power of the Spirit in our mortal bodies.

But this still leaves us with another question. What is really happening when people claim to be baptised in the Spirit some time after their conversion? The answer, I believe, is as follows: they are simply beginning to experience what they received when they were born again. They are experiencing a release of what was given when they confessed Jesus as Lord. They are experiencing an awakening of affections or feelings which have been dormant since their Christian birth. They are actualising and appropriating **NOW** what was actually given **THEN**.

What many believe is a subsequent baptism in the Spirit is, in reality, best described in terms of liberation. It is a breakthrough experience in which the charismatic and experiential dimension of Christianity is liberated from the realm of the unconscious into the conscious life of the believer. It is the first awareness at the perceptual level of the power of the Spirit given at Christian initiation. As Michael Green puts it, in his book *Baptism, Its Purpose, Practice and Power* (Hodder & Stoughton, 1987):

> Maybe 'release' in the Spirit is a good term. What happens, of course, is that we discover in actual experience what had been there potentially all the time in our baptism. It is a case of **possessing our possessions**. (p.136)

That seems to me to be right. What many mistakenly believe is

Spirit baptism is really the liberation of the dove who was caged at conversion. Sooner or later, most of us unlock the cage and allow the dove of the Spirit to fly in an unrestricted way. When that happens, we start to experience something of the fullness of our inheritance in Christ Jesus.

6

Preparation

If the view taken in this book is right (and you will need to test it), then we must prepare new converts to be baptised in the Holy Spirit. If baptism in the Holy Spirit is a powerful immersion in the supernatural power of God during our conversion, then we must take steps to help people to experience this watershed event then and not later! The secret is to help folk to be 'ready'.

In this final chapter, I will use the letters of the word R-E-A-D-Y to highlight five vital ways in which you can prepare to be baptised in the Holy Spirit. Obviously we must exercise caution here. We must remember that we do not initiate special experiences of the Spirit, God does. We must also keep in mind that the Spirit is not controlled by neat techniques. If these caveats are observed, then the following suggestions will be of help to you.

R is for REPENT

You cannot be baptised in the Spirit until you have repented of your sins and confessed Jesus as Lord. In other words, you must renounce all involvement with things that are contrary to God's Word, and you must turn from a self-centred to a God-centred life. Furthermore, you must believe in your heart that Jesus is risen from the dead and confess with your lips that Jesus is Lord (Romans 10:9). You must acknowledge the uniqueness, the ultimacy and the deity of Jesus of Nazareth. When you have done those things, then you may ask the Lord Jesus to baptise you with his Holy Spirit. Open your heart to the Spirit and receive what the Father has promised. God will answer that prayer.

In practical terms, you will need to repent of any sin that might hinder the power of the Spirit in your life. God's Spirit is called the **Holy** Spirit. In at least one passage of Scripture, he is called *'the spirit of holiness'* (Romans 1:4). If there is any immorality in your life, repent of it. That means, put it to death (Colossians 3:5). If you have had any involvement in the occult, renounce it. As Peter says in Acts 5:32, the Holy Spirit is given to those who obey God.

True repentance often involves drastic steps. One friend of mine recognised this and burnt all his papers to do with freemasonry in his open fire (see Acts 19:18-12). The fire was so strong that it buckled the grate! However, that act was the prelude to him being filled with the Spirit and speaking in tongues! Clearly it was very important to the Holy Spirit.

Repentance is therefore a crucial preparation for experiencing the fullness of the Holy Spirit. Indeed, a spring clean of our lives is essential if we are to be baptised in the Holy Spirit.

E is for EXPECT

It is important, secondly, to change your mind if you have not expected the Holy Spirit to be a part of the normal Christian life. You need to expect God to give you the gift and the gifts! They are for the passionate, not for the passive! As the great theologian Karl Barth once said, 'Only where the Spirit is sighed, cried and prayed for does He become present and newly active'.

The dimension of faith-expectancy is crucial here. In Galatians 3:2, Paul asks,

> *'Did you receive the Spirit by observing the Law or by believing what you heard?'*

In these words, Paul shows that we receive the Spirit by faith, not by works (by believing in the Word not by observing rules).

Faith is therefore vital. Expecting the Holy Spirit to come is an essential preparation for Spirit baptism. It is an act of faith on our part. It shows that we are taking God's Word seriously and that we believe his promises, not least the promise of his Holy Spirit.

Perhaps it is here that we have a lot to learn from the

Pentecostals. They have always stressed the need to tarry or wait for the Holy Spirit. Many of their hymns exhort people to expect the Spirit:

> Bring your empty earthen vessels,
> Clean thru' Jesus' precious blood,
> Come, ye needy, one and all;
> And in human consecration wait
> Before the throne of God
> Till the Holy Ghost shall fall.

Whilst I do not recommend a return to the excesses of the old 'tarrying meetings', I do recommend expectant and patient waiting. That is a vital part of our preparation.

A is for ASK

Jesus says,

> *'A-sk and you will receive*
> *S-eek and you will find*
> *K-nock and the door will be opened.'*

In Luke's gospel, this saying is uttered just before Jesus talks about asking for the gift of the Spirit:

> *'Which of you fathers, if your son asks for a fish, will give him a snake instead? Or if he asks for an egg, will give him a scorpion? If you, then, though you are evil, know how to give good gifts to your children, how much more will your Father in heaven give the Holy Spirit to those who ask him!'*
>
> (Luke 11:9-13)

In Luke and Acts, asking for the Holy Spirit in prayer is a crucial act of faith. I have already underlined the distinctive way in which Luke shows Jesus praying at his baptism in the River Jordan. It was *'as he was praying'* that the Spirit came down upon

Jesus (Luke 3:22). Luke continues this theme in Acts. It is as the 120 disciples are all together in prayer that the Spirit descends upon them (Acts 1:14; 2:1). It as the 3,120 disciples are in prayer that the Spirit fills them again in Acts 4:23-31 (sometimes referred to as the second Pentecost). Clearly Luke sees asking in prayer as a pre-requisite for receiving the gift and the gifts of the Spirit.

Note one thing, however. The tenses in Luke 11:9-10 are present continuous. Jesus literally says, 'Go on asking... Go on seeking... Go on knocking!' If knocking on the door does not work the first time, do not give up. Take encouragement from the persistent widow in Luke 18:1-8. Keep knocking on heaven's door!

D is for DRINK

You will have noticed by now that the New Testament writers, when they talk about the Holy Spirit, cannot resist liquid images. They speak of the Holy Spirit as water. They speak of this Spirit being poured out from heaven. They speak of believers drinking the Spirit. Liquid images abound in the New Testament.

A fourth way of preparing for baptism in the Holy Spirit is by obeying Jesus' words in John 7:37:

'If any man is thirsty, let him come to me and drink'.

It is important to stand under the waterfall of grace with your mouth open, not shut!

Not long ago a friend of mine was given a vision by the Lord. It was of a great waterfall cascading down onto a large flat rock. On this rock, there were a lot of people with umbrellas. Some had their umbrellas up and were trying to keep dry. Others had their umbrellas up but, from time to time, were peeping out from underneath to see what the water was like. Others had thrown their umbrellas away and were literally dancing in the waterfall, drinking quaffs of water, having a whale of a time.

It goes without saying that a person preparing to be filled with the Holy Spirit is best off without an umbrella! *'God gives the Spirit without limit'* (John 3:34).

Y is for YIELD

Finally, yield your life to the Holy Spirit. Let go of your control over your life and hand it over to the Holy Spirit. Give the Spirit permission to do what he wants with you. Allow yourself *'to be controlled by the Spirit'* (Romans 8:9). Allow yourself to be led by the Spirit (Romans 8:14; Galatians 3:18). Make it your aim to live by the Spirit and to keep in step with the promptings of the Spirit rather than the inclinations of the flesh. Become open to a discipleship which manifests 'demonstrations of the Spirit's power' (1 Corinthians 2:4; Romans 15:18-19; Hebrews 2:4).

Remember, As Michael Cassidy once put it, that 'our fullness in the Holy Spirit is in proportion to the degree of our surrender. *We are as full of the Holy Spirit as our surrender.'*

Summary

So repent, expect, ask, drink and yield. These are key acts of preparation as far as baptism in the Holy Spirit is concerned. Sooner rather than later, the Spirit will fill you to overflowing.

What, finally, of the experience itself? What happens when you are actually baptised in the Spirit? How does it happen? Where?

This experience may occur on your own, riding a bike, praying in your bedroom, even washing-up! I have heard of many stories like that. On the other hand, it may come in a time of ministry in which trusted, charismatic friends pray for you with the laying on of hands.

It may come in an instant and last a few minutes or hours. On the other hand it may happen more gradually, more as a process than a crisis.

It may be dramatic, with heat going through your whole body and gifts such as tongues and prophecy being immediately evident. On the other hand, it may be incredibly gentle – more a matter of inner peace than of immense power.

There is no one form of being baptised in the Holy Spirit. The Spirit of God is sovereign and he deals with us all in different ways. He is like the desert wind in ancient Palestine, that blows where it wants (John 3:8). He is mysterious, elusive and unfathomable. We cannot control him by our tidy doctrines and rigorous systems of thought. He comes to us, but he comes on his own terms, according to his own timetable, and in his own way. All he asks is that we wait and that we wait with humility, with dependence and with openness.

As Jesus said, *'Wait for the gift my Father promised!'* (Acts 1:4).

Post-Script

I would like to end with a warning. Through this book I have stressed the importance of operating in the power of the Spirit, of experiencing the fullness of the Spirit. We need to be thoroughly baptised in the Spirit at our conversion, and we need to go on being filled with the Holy Spirit throughout our lives (Ephesians 5:18). Having said that, we must be very careful not to turn experience of the Spirit into an end in itself. There are many people today who worship worship instead of the one we are called to worship. There are many who have got locked into a worldly addiction to spiritual experience – who are looking for a high from the Spirit. This grieves the Spirit, for God never intended us to receive charismatic power for comfort, self-indulgence and superficiality, but rather for holiness, mission, and maturity. It is a sad fact that this should need underlining so firmly in our own times.

In my opinion, the final word must be the word 'obedience'. In Matthew's version of Jesus' baptism in the Spirit, this word seems to me to be very important. If Matthew has a distinctive view on baptism in the Holy Spirit it seems to me to be about obedience. Matthew (unlike the other gospel writers) tells us that Jesus accepted baptism at the hands of John the Baptist to fulfil all righteousness (Matthew 3:15); i.e. because the Father had told him to! It was an act of obedience. The first verse after the baptism account shows the Spirit leading Jesus out into the desert to be tempted by the devil (Matthew 4:1). The Spirit comes upon Jesus at his baptism, but then leads Jesus into a place where his personal obedience will be sorely tested. As far as Jesus is concerned, Matthew says that his baptism in the Spirit was a result of his obedience and resulted in obedience!

Matthew's special view of Spirit baptism therefore seems to be about obedience, holiness and righteousness. Matthew is not impressed with Christians who have spiritual power but no holiness. He is the only one to record Jesus' rather disturbing remark:

'Not everyone who says to me, "Lord, Lord" will enter the Kingdom of heaven, but only he who does the will of my Father who is in heaven. Many will say to me on that day, "Lord, Lord, did we not prophesy in your name, and in your name drive out demons and perform many miracles?" Then I will tell them plainly, "I never knew you. Away from me, you evildoers".' (Matthew 7:21-23)

My feeling is that Matthew was having problems in his own church with people who wanted the gifts but not the fruit, the power but not the holiness, the charisma but not the character. He was disturbed enough by this tendency to include a warning of Jesus concerning the priority of obedience over miracles. He reports Jesus' saying that it is he who does the will of the Father who can be certain of heaven, not the one who relies purely on supernatural manifestations. Furthermore, he seems to emphasise the relationship between baptism in the Spirit and personal obedience. To be sure, Jesus' baptism results in powerful, charismatic ministry. Matthew, like Mark and Luke, still agrees with that view. But he also insists that baptism in the Spirit is empowerment for a holy, righteous life. That is why he alone records Jesus' saying:

'All authority in heaven and on earth has been given to me. Therefore, go and make disciples of all nations, baptising them in the name of the Father, the Son and the Holy Spirit, and teaching them to obey everything I have commanded you'. (Matthew 28:18-19)

What could be clearer than that? Baptism, says Jesus, must be followed by total obedience. Once the disciples have fully initiated believers into the Kingdom (*'baptising them in the name of the Father, the Son and the Holy Spirit'*) they are then to teach them how to live a righteous life which, to quote Matthew 5:20, exceeds that of the Pharisees (*'teaching them to obey everything I have commanded you'*). Obedience must follow baptism!

Perhaps this is a word for all Pentecostals and neo-Pentecostals. Not all of us have emphasised holiness as much as power. Not all of us have sought God's righteousness as much as his dynamic, charismatic Kingdom (Matthew 6:33). It may be that Matthew's view of Spirit-baptism has a lot to teach us about spiritual maturity, about growing on from a fascination with experience to an integration of righteous lifestyle with supernatural power.

That may or may not be the case. I leave the reader to discern and to decide. One thing I do know is that baptism in the Spirit is part of what David Pawson calls the normal Christian birth, and that being filled with the Spirit is part of that Watchman Nee called the normal Christian life! We are to receive the Spirit in power during our conversion and initiation into the Kingdom of God. That is what is meant by being baptised in the Spirit. But then we are to go on being filled with the power of the Holy Spirit after that (Ephesians 5:18). That is what is meant by remaining *'full of the Holy Spirit'* (Acts 6:3, 7:55, etc).

My prayer is that we who confess Jesus as Lord will know in our hearts as well as in our heads that power for sonship, service and sacrifice which is released through baptism in the Holy Spirit. Such power would truly renew the church and reform society. Nothing is more urgent than that. So, as we approach the beginning of the 21st century, may we all pray the prayer prayed by William Arthur in 1856:

> And now, adorable Spirit, proceeding from the Father and the Son, descend upon all the churches, renew the Pentecost in this our age, and baptise Thy people generally – O baptise them yet again with tongues of fire! Crown this... century with a revival of 'pure and undefiled religion' greater than that of the last century, greater than any 'demonstration of the Spirit' even yet vouchsafed to men!

And **all** the Lord's people said, "Amen!"

APPENDIX:
The Role of the Spirit in Conversion, According to the Pentecostals.

Many readers of this booklet will no doubt be wondering how Pentecostals and neo-Pentecostals can separate regeneration (being born again) from receiving the gift of the Spirit (Spirit baptism). How can such believers distinguish between a first blessing (in which we do not receive the Spirit) and a second blessing (in which we do receive him)? Surely the Holy Spirit is involved in our regeneration? Surely he (the Holy Spirit) evokes the repentance of sin and faith in Christ which constitute our rebirth?

It is worth just briefly turning to Don Basham's book, *A Handbook on Holy Spirit Baptism*, for guidance here – not least because it is the bestselling Pentecostal work on our subject (300,000 copies in print). In chapter 5, Don addresses the following question: 'I had a wonderful conversion experience and assumed I received the Holy Spirit then. Doesn't conversion bring the Holy Spirit?'

Don's answer is interesting. He concedes that the Holy Spirit is involved in our conversion, because Paul states that no one can say 'Jesus is Lord!' except by the Holy Spirit. However, he also categorically dismisses the idea that we receive the gift of the Spirit then and there. That is reserved for later, when we are given spiritual power. This reception of charismatic power is a 'deeper experience of the Holy Spirit' which 'opens unto us a whole new realm of spiritual possibilities'. This experience of power is baptism in the Holy Spirit.

In order to explain the role of the Spirit in these two blessings (regeneration and Spirit baptism), Don Basham turns to a favourite illustration of Rev. Dennis Bennett, author of *Nine O'Clock in the Morning*. Dennis Bennett used to put it thus: in our conversion, the Holy Spirit is like a man who pushes past my secretary and sits in my office whilst I am still busily working at my desk. He sits there whilst I continue my business. He is there but I am unaware of him. It is only the secretary ringing my office which tells me that the man has arrived.

Baptism in the Spirit (the second blessing) is like what happens next. I lay aside my work and give the visitor a cordial welcome, devoting my undivided attention to his presence and to his needs. The visitor stands up and says, 'I'm so happy you've finally *received* me. Here's a cheque for one million pounds and it's made out to you. Furthermore, there's an important message from a friend of mine, and that is that there are many other good things for you to have, *now that you have received me*'.

Like Dennis Bennett, Don Basham uses this analogy to explain the role of the Spirit in regeneration and in Holy Spirit baptism. A person who has been born again but not baptised in the Holy Spirit is like the first stage of the illustration above. The visitor is in the office, but the man working at the desk has not welcomed him. We *have* the Holy Spirit in our lives but we have not *received* him. However, when we are baptised in the Holy Spirit, we move on to the second stage of the illustration. We have now made the Spirit fully welcome, and we now give him our full attention. We have now *received* him.

The use of this illustration is very revealing. What is so interesting to my mind is that is really only works if you have the kind of understanding of Spirit baptism which I have described in this book – which is not Pentecostal. In my book, I have argued that we receive the gift of the Spirit at our conversion, but that many of us only wake up to his presence much later. Many of us only possess our charismatic possessions at a subsequent date. This, interestingly, is exactly what happens in Dennis Bennett's famous illustration. We have the visitor in the office, but we have not yet awoken to his presence or to his 'presents'! We have the Spirit, but we have not yet fully welcomed him.

If you take the Pentecostal view of Spirit baptism, there are real difficulties with this illustration. Pentecostals claim that the Spirit is involved in our conversion but we have not received him! But how can that be? How can the Spirit be at work in my heart producing godly sorrow over my sin and deep faith in Jesus, and yet at the same time remain 'unreceived'? Either he is in me or he is not! There is no difference, to my mind, between *having* and *receiving*. If he is in the office, he is in the office!

The main difference is not between 'having' and 'receiving', but between 'receiving' and 'recognising'. The overall teaching of the New Testament supports the view that we 'receive' the Holy Spirit when we repent of sin and confess Jesus as Lord (i.e. during our initiation into the Kingdom) but that many of us only 'recognise' his power and his gifts at a later date – for reasons which I have described in this book. That later 'awakening' is often such a dramatic experience that folk interpret it as a watershed event – as baptism in the Spirit. But really it is a release of what is already there, in tremendous power and with unmistakable supernatural consequences.

In conclusion, then, I do believe that it is wrong to pray for baptism in the Spirit if we have already been born again. Being born again involves baptism in the Spirit. What many of us need to pray for today is for a dramatic release of that Spirit. Or, if we received the Spirit *in power* at our conversion (which many do), we need to pray that God would fill us again! That seems to me to be an approach which marries both Word and Spirit – and how that marriage is needed in our day.